U.S. Fish & Wildlife Service

NATIONAL
WILDLIFE
REFUGE
SYSTEM

June 2013
Final Report:

A Landscape-Scale Approach to Refuge System Planning

The Refuge System can be a catalyst for change throughout the greater conservation planning community and become a primary partner in advancing the Service's conservation design efforts.

Final Report:

A Landscape-Scale Approach to Refuge System Planning

Table of Contents

Introduction

The Planning Implementation Team (PIT) was chartered to address this recommendation from Conserving the Future: Wildlife Refuges and the Next Generation, the U.S. Fish and Wildlife Service's 21st century strategic vision for the National Wildlife Refuge System. Our charge was to investigate how Refuge System planning will address large-scale conservation challenges such as climate change, while maintaining the integrity of management and conservation delivery within our boundaries.

This report is our proposal for "A Landscape-Scale Approach to Refuge System Planning." It recommends that we focus the next generation of planning on Landscape Conservation Designs (LCDs), developed by the greater conservation community through partnership in Landscape Conservation Cooperatives (LCCs). LCDs are consistent with Strategic Habitat Conservation (SHC) and are a partnership-driven conservation strategy that identifies desired future conditions and management prescriptions at multiple scales across jurisdictions. Key to our recommendation is incorporating LCDs into the preplanning phase of every Comprehensive Conservation Plan (CCP) and Land Protection Plan (LPP). With limited exceptions, no CCP or LPP should be developed until after an LCD has been completed. We envision that LCDs would include multiple refuges within

a defined geographic area that leads to a single, broader CCP with step-down management plans to address site-specific management.

Many refuges already employ a landscape-scale conservation approach, but we need to increase these efforts and incorporate the LCD approach across the entire Refuge System. The Refuge System can be a catalyst for change throughout the greater conservation planning community and become a primary partner in the LCC network's design efforts. We also need to incorporate and more clearly communicate biological, social, and economic science into Refuge System plans at all scales.

In addition to recommending an approach for landscape-scale planning, the report also addresses: CCP revisions and amendments, plan schedules and tracking, standardized templates, and some policy changes required to fully implement these recommendations. While some of the strategies will result in streamlining and efficiencies, others require more technical expertise, training, and staff.

Our recommendations apply only to the Refuge System, but it is our hope that other Service programs join us in basing their program-specific management plans on LCDs.

"Incorporate the lessons learned from our first round of CCPs and HMPs into the next generation of conservation plans, and ensure these new plans view refuges in a landscape context and describe actions to project conservation benefits beyond refuge boundaries."

- from *Recommendation One* in *Conserving the Future: Wildlife Refuges and the Next Generation.*

Getting Started

Conserving the Future offers a series of recommendations that address important issues including Recommendation 1, for which the PIT is responsible. Charged with developing the next generation of conservation plans in a broader, landscape context, the PIT began by developing a Work Plan consisting of tasks that addressed specific issues. Over the past two years we:

• held a number of meetings, and enlisted the help of others in the Refuge System and across the Service, representatives from other federal agencies, the Association of Fish and Wildlife Agencies, and a number of non-governmental conservation organizations;

• surveyed refuge staff to determine how planning processes could be improved, adapted, or streamlined while further integrating refuges into the landscape matrix; and

• reviewed completed CCPs, previous studies of CCPs, past planning recommendations, and other agencies' and organizations' conservation planning models.

This work resulted in a large collection of reports, survey data, reference tools, and analyses that form a Report Compendium of planning resources. It is from this variety of contributors, data, and analyses that we draw our recommendations.

Opportunities, Challenges, and Action

The Refuge System is the world's largest collection of lands and waters specifically designated and managed for fish and wildlife. Overall, it provides habitat for more than 700 species of birds, 220 species of mammals, 250 reptile and amphibian species, 200 species of fish, and more than 280 threatened or endangered plants and animals. Conservation planning is essential for ensuring that the Refuge System knows where it's going and meets its commitment to conserving fish, wildlife, plants, and their

There are over 560 National Wildlife Refuges; photo: USFWS

habitats for future generations of Americans. Today, planning is done primarily through CCPs, which drive on-the-ground management on refuges across the country. CCPs identify goals and objectives for refuge management and identify strategies to achieve these goals and objectives. The Service is nearing the completion of a CCP for every unit of the Refuge System. Some units have started to revise their original CCP, and many have also begun work on documents such as the Habitat Management Plan (HMP) that "step down" the guidance of CCPs to a greater level of specificity.

Up to now, many CCPs have identified landscape-scale conservation goals and are translating these into management actions that can be implemented on a refuge. To be effective in confronting the challenges posed by climate change, invasive species, and habitat fragmentation the next generation of plans must continue this effort and broaden our focus beyond refuge boundaries. We must tie refuge planning and management actions to the larger landscape. These plans must also incorporate the best available science, encourage collaboration with partners, be readable, and inspire action. The challenge is to define clear priorities for wildlife conservation within landscapes and to implement larger-scale conservation with multiple and perhaps, unconventional partners.

See a list of compendium content provided at the back of this report or the complete *Report Compendium* of planning resources on *SharePoint*.

Major Recommendations

- Promote LCDs throughout the Service, LCCs, and the greater conservation planning community.

- Develop LCDs as part of the preplanning phase of every refuge-specific CCP and LPP.

- Postpone developing new CCPs and LPPs and revising existing CCPs and LPPs until after first completing corresponding LCDs. Continue completing step-down plans needed to implement existing CCPs in the interim.

- Include in a single CCP, when possible, all refuges within the geographic area covered by the LCD.

- Consolidate to the maximum extent feasible, step-down management plans for all refuges within the geographic area covered by an LCD.

- Base refuge-specific plans on LCDs to help ensure that every plan relies on sound biological, social, and economic science.

- Strive to develop CCPs in a broad scope with more details provided in step-down management plans.

- Prioritize the completion of HMPs and visitor services plans.

- Modify the Refuge Annual Performance Plan (RAPP) database to geospatially track every refuge's progress in implementing CCPs and contributing towards LCDs.

- Incorporate CCP implementation into the Annual Performance Plans of refuge managers, project leaders, and refuge supervisors.

- Clearly communicate in Refuge System plans how the best available science was used to develop specific and measurable goals, objectives, and strategies.

- Develop standardized templates for new CCPs, LPPs, and step-down management plans.

- Revise policies and training to fully implement these recommendations.

- Evaluate the Refuge System's planning organization, capacity to conduct landscape-level planning, and budget—if and when we move forward with the recommendations contained in this final report.

> *"Landscape Conservation Design is an important part of achieving SHC's purpose."*

Landscape Conservation Design: In Support of SHC

In 2006, Service leadership endorsed Strategic Habitat Conservation as the adaptive management approach it would use to achieve its mission in the 21st century. In response to the unprecedented scale and complexity of challenges facing our natural resources, there was a need to develop and implement a landscape approach to conservation that was more strategic, science-driven, collaborative, adaptive, and understandable.

SHC is a response to changes affecting not only the Service but the conservation community at large. It allows the Service to deal with issues of scale and accountability and effectively work with our partners to address priorities and challenges such as climate change. The purpose of SHC is to coordinate and link actions that various Service programs and partners perform at individual sites so that their combined effect may be capable of achieving these outcomes at the larger landscape, regional, or continental scales. Landscape Conservation Design is an important part of achieving SHC's purpose.

SHC (exhibit A) is built on five main elements: (1) Biological planning – working with partners to identify conservation features (e.g., surrogate species), measurable targets for those features (i.e., population objectives), and the limiting factors affecting them; (2) Conservation design – creating tools that help to identify and

direct conservation actions effectively and efficiently towards a desired future condition; (3) Conservation delivery – working collaboratively with partners to carry out conservation strategies on-the-ground; (4) Outcome-based monitoring – evaluating the effectiveness of conservation actions in achieving desired future conditions and to adapt future

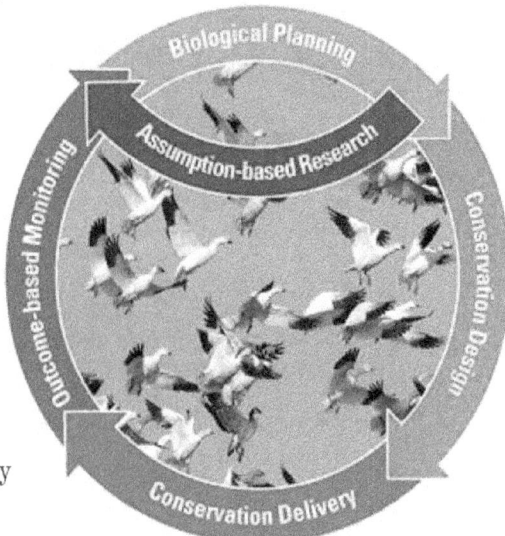

Exhibit A: The U.S. Fish and Wildlife Service's Strategic Habitat Conservation Framework

planning and delivery; and (5) Assumption driven research – testing assumptions made during biological planning and conservation design to refine future plans and actions.

In the spirit of SHC, and with the intent of fulfilling its conservation design element, LCD stands as a partnership-driven method to assess current and anticipated future conditions (biological and socioeconomic), offers a spatially-explicit depiction of a desired future condition, and helps provide management prescriptions for achieving those conditions. LCD is both a process and a product.

In creating an LCD, each partner identifies the conservation features within their purview (such as the Service' surrogate species and the Refuge System's strategic growth priorities). This is, in effect, the biological planning portion of SHC. Collectively, these features are used to define the geographic extent of the LCD, develop conservation targets (such as population objectives) within that landscape, identify limiting factors (i.e., threats and stressors such as climate change), conduct gap and population analyses, and model future resource relationships. The partners then identify management, restoration, and protection strategies that can be implemented to address the identified resource concerns, attain desired future conditions, sustain ecosystem function, and achieve the missions, mandates, and goals of each partner organization. Upon completion of the LCD, partners implement the strategies applicable to their organization. Normally, this would require each individual partner to conduct more detailed, site-specific planning (such as Refuge CCPs and LPPs) prior to implementation. Over time, partners monitor and evaluate the effectiveness of their individual and collective implementation and reconvene to assess and revise the LCD on a periodic basis.

Attributes of an LCD are listed in table 1 followed by some of the key features described in more detail.

LCDs are developed and delivered with our partners.
The greater conservation community's engagement in LCDs is essential, because the Service's ability to fulfill its conservation mission relies on its partners in delivering the on-the-ground design. An LCD is an assessment of the landscape's current and potential future condition, a description of a desired future condition, and a suite of preliminary, coarse-scale management strategies that are developed by the greater conservation community. Coarse-scale landscape goals and objectives and a suite

Table 1: Attributes of an LCD

LCD initiation and development are dependent on the greater conservation community's collaborative efforts.
Conservation partners voluntarily combine their processes, data, tools, technical capacity, and other resources to create an LCD.
LCDs include biological and socioeconomic assessments of current conditions.
Current threats and stressors are assessed as part of an LCD.
LCDs employ models to describe potential future conditions under various scenarios.
An LCD is neither an individual partner's management plan nor a decision-document that requires National Environmental Policy Act (NEPA) compliance.
LCDs inform the development of each partner's site-specific management plans (and NEPA compliance documents) within the landscape described by the LCD.
LCDs are peer-reviewed.
LCDs provide information for the greater conservation community that would not have been cost-effective for each partner to obtain alone.
LCDs facilitate discussion about collaborative conservation at the landscape scale.
An LCD's success is evaluated based on each partner's implementation and monitoring of the strategies identified in their individual management plans.
LCDs require periodic revision based on changing conditions, the availability of new data, and/or the results of each partner's implementation and monitoring of management actions.
LCDs catalyze the achievement of the greater conservation community's missions, goals, and objectives.

of broad strategies can inform or guide development of each agency's or organization's site-specific management plans.

LCDs are based on sound science. An LCD relies on the collaboration of the greater conservation community in bringing together the diversity of frameworks, processes, data, tools, technical capabilities, and other resources that each partner agency and organization possess—and which are needed—to accurately assess and address the current and future condition of the landscape. This collaborative approach distributes the burden of developing and implementing the design across the greater conservation community and improves coordination between partners. Following the SHC framework, an LCD is based on the greater conservation community's ability to identify conservation features of particular interest. The Service's surrogate species approach to planning is one example. An LCD identifies coarse-scale targets for those features, such as population objectives, and it articulates key assumptions. Limiting factors (i.e., threats and stressors) and future research needs are identified as well. An LCD also conducts other key science-based activities that are of particular interest, such as: climate modeling, vulnerability assessments, land use including infrastructure analyses, and socioeconomic impact analyses.

LCDs are technologically advanced. An LCD utilizes the latest in geospatial technologies to aid decision makers in understanding both present-day and future trends and conditions. Technologies, including Geographic Information Systems (GIS), remote sensing, and spatial modeling are used to assess and evaluate both current conditions and expected changes to physical and socioeconomic parameters such as climate, land use, population and demographics, transportation, and energy infrastructure. Data development, modeling, and the creation of decision support tools are expected to be collaborative outputs of an LCD. An LCD may include gap analyses, population viability analyses, and other models that depict future resource relationships.

LCDs are iterative. An LCD is not a static product. It must be periodically modified by all partners based on the results of their collective implementation, monitoring, and evaluation. This is adaptive management at a landscape scale.

The LCCs' Role in LCD Development

The Service is committed to taking a collaborative, science-driven, landscape-scale conservation approach to achieve its mission. This commitment is exemplified by the Service's endorsement of the SHC framework in 2006 and Landscape Conservation Cooperatives in 2009. Ken Salazar, Secretary of the Interior signed *Secretarial Order No. 3289* on September 14, 2009, which officially established the LCCs.

Twenty-two LCCs collectively form a national network. The network's vision is to preserve "landscapes capable of sustaining natural and cultural resources for current and future generations." The network's role for achieving that vision is, in part, to provide a forum for national and international conservation planning and to facilitate and integrate efforts across and among the individual LCCs.

In November 2011 sixty leaders from the conservation community representing non-profit organizations, state and federal agencies, and others met to discuss the potential for substantially and strategically improving the Nation's system of wildlife habitats as described in the Wildlife Habitat Policy Research Program's (WHPRP) *2010 research report*. The report recommended that LCCs be a forum to "identify and map conservation priorities at multiple scales to guide investments in habitat protection, management, and restoration." In July 2012 the Service released *"DRAFT Guidance on Selecting Species for Design of Landscape-scale Conservation,"* which states that LCCs were "established to support biological planning and conservation design at landscape scales" and suggests that LCC partnership efforts "should continue and be expanded . . . to integrate priorities and select common targets to be used for designing the conservation of sustainable landscapes."

Many of the 22 LCCs have identified LCD as a priority in their strategic, operational, and/or science needs plans. Some have initiated development of LCD components (e.g., decision support tool development) and others have sponsored LCD development. These initial LCDs (listed in table 2) will serve as national pilot projects that can be used to identify and duplicate effective processes.

The PIT supports the LCC network's vision and purpose and supports the WHPRP LCC-related recommendation described above. We assert that the Refuge System should be an advocate for the LCC network's interest in designing functional landscapes, be a catalyst for change throughout the greater conservation planning community through leading by example, and become a primary partner in the LCC network's design efforts.

The Refuge System's Role in LCD Development

Although the network of LCC partnerships is still relatively new, it has made exceptional progress in building a national and regional organizational framework, internal capacity, partnerships, and support. LCC partnerships have successfully identified their collective science needs and have begun to develop products to address those needs including those related to LCD. To ensure that LCC-sponsored LCDs are relevant to Refuge System interests, the Refuge System should immediately engage in those efforts at the national level and with each LCC.

The PIT recognizes that Refuge System planners and other staff possess significant professional skills and attributes that could contribute to the LCCs' development of LCDs. They include partnership building, facilitation, project and contract management, obtaining resource-specific information and expertise, data collection and management, GIS modeling and analysis, writing and editing, and document design. The Refuge System could become a catalyst for LCD

Table 2: LCC-Sponsored LCDs and/or Products that Support LCD Development

Project	LCC	FWS Region	Geographic Context
Arid Lands Initiative/Collaborative Conservation Assessment and Prioritization	Great Northern	1	Columbia Plateau Ecoregion
Big Bend-Río Bravo Collaboration for Trans-boundary Landscape Conservation	Desert	2	Big Bend-Rio Bravo Region
Breeding Bird Distribution and Abundance Influenced by Climate and Land Cover Change	Upper Midwest and Great Lakes	3	LCC-wide Geography
South Atlantic LCC Conservation Blueprint	South Atlantic	4	LCC-wide Geography
Eastern North Carolina/Southeastern Virginia SHC Team Strategic Plan	South Atlantic	4–5	Roanoke-Tar-Neuse-Cape Fear Ecosystem
Designing Sustainable Landscapes	North Atlantic	5	LCC-wide Geography
Regional Assessment of Fish Habitat Condition	Plains and Prairie Potholes	6	Northern Great Plains
Assessment of Land Status and Protection Levels	Northwest Boreal	7	Northwest Boreal Ecoregion
Conservation Lands Network	California	8	San Francisco Bay Watershed

> *"... working in partnership with the greater conservation community will result in a higher quality plan, a holistic view of the landscape, and a greater capacity for conservation delivery."*

development by directing some of this expertise to the LCCs.

Working within the LCCs' collaborative framework may require more time than if the Refuge System were to take a "go-it-alone" approach to LCD development. But working in partnership with the greater conservation community will result in a higher quality plan, a holistic view of the landscape, and a greater capacity for conservation delivery. Furthermore, the product resulting from a collaborative approach will provide the Refuge System, other Service programs, and the greater conservation community with information that will help us to collectively better understand our individual role in delivering conservation as the landscape around us changes with time. While refuge staff must be engaged and provide input in LCD development, the bulk of the design work will be conducted through the partnerships formed around LCDs and fostered through the LCCs. In the long-term, this collaborative approach will save each partner time and resources. For example, rather than a refuge developing a climate vulnerability assessment on their own, an LCD will provide the necessary climate science and predictive decision support tools to assess the vulnerabilities of multiple refuges. In this way, LCDs will bring new economies of scale in developing refuge-specific plans.

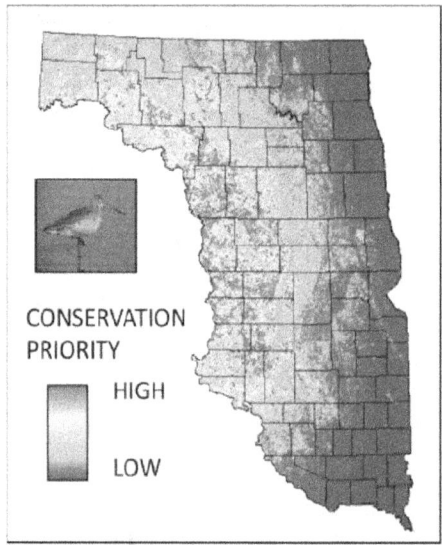

CONSERVATION PRIORITY

HIGH

LOW

Photo: USFWS

Refuge System planning is conducted in two phases: an assessment and design phase followed by development of an implementation strategy (exhibit B). Refuge System policy identifies these two phases as "preplanning" and "planning." We recommend that LCDs be developed as part of the preplanning phase of every refuge-specific CCP and LPP. (The PIT recognizes that additional preplanning, beyond the LCD, will normally be required for each refuge-specific plan in order to address site-specific issues.) We further recommend postponing the development of refuge-specific CCPs and LPPs until the completion of the corresponding LCD. The

Exhibit B:
Two Phases of Planning

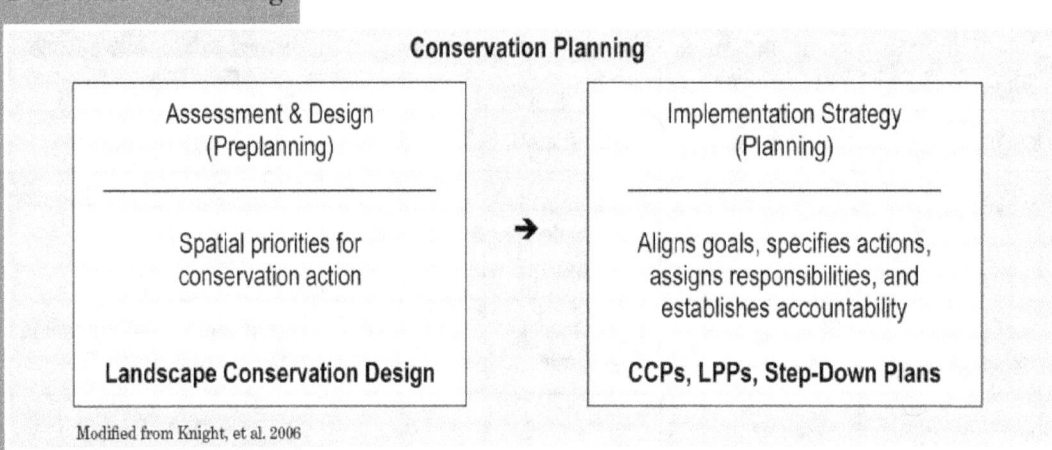

Conservation Planning

Assessment & Design (Preplanning)		Implementation Strategy (Planning)
Spatial priorities for conservation action	→	Aligns goals, specifies actions, assigns responsibilities, and establishes accountability
Landscape Conservation Design		**CCPs, LPPs, Step-Down Plans**

Modified from Knight, et al. 2006

completion of step-down management plans needed to implement existing CCPs should continue in the interim.

LCD will provide an opportunity for the Refuge System to streamline our land protection planning process. Our current process consists of two phases: preliminary planning and detailed planning. These two phases are equivalent to the preplanning and planning phases described above. Preliminary planning results in the development of a Preliminary Project Proposal (PPP), which, with the Director's approval, is followed by a detailed planning process that results in the development of an LPP.

The PIT recommends that land protection strategies developed after completion of LCDs replace PPPs, because an LCD will include a more comprehensive assessment of a potential new refuge (or refuge expansion) than is currently provided by a PPP. Director approval of the land protection strategies in an LCD will be required to enter detailed planning. In addition, an LCD will allow the Refuge System to reassess the value of any previously-approved LPPs that occur within that geographic area. We recommend that this assessment be conducted as part of each LCD that contains areas proposed for new or expanded refuges.

Recommendations

- Do not develop or revise, with limited exceptions, any refuge-specific CCP or LPP until after the corresponding LCD has been developed in cooperation with our conservation partners in an LCC.
- Postpone developing new CCPs and LPPs and revising existing CCPs and LPPs until after first completing corresponding LCDs. Continuing completing step-down management plans needed to implement existing CCPs in the interim.
- Develop LCDs as part of the preplanning phase of every refuge-specific CCP and LPP.
- Design refuge-specific CCPs, LPPs, and step-down management plans to both address refuge-specific issues and implement the landscape-level goals and objectives identified in the corresponding LCD.
- Use information and strategies from LCDs in place of currently required PPPs to inform and prioritize LPP development.
- Reassess, upon completion of an LCD, the value and contribution of previously-approved LPPs within that geographic area.
- Incorporate feedback, by LCDs, from refuges and other conservation partners to enhance and inform landscape design through adaptive management.
- Promote LCDs within the Service by:
    - assigning a Headquarters LCD Coordinator and regional office LCD Coordinators;
    - developing institutional structures, processes, and protocols that facilitate effective communications between Service programs, LCCs, and other conservation partners;
    - directing national and regional level capacity towards the coordination of Service-wide interests in LCD; and
    - advocating for and supporting the development of a Service-wide LCD policy.
- Promote LCDs throughout the greater conservation planning community by:
    - communicating the concept, use, and values of LCDs;
    - advocating for design integration amongst LCC partners;
    - being an early adopter of integration by directing capacity to each of the 22 LCCs in support of LCD development; and
    - promoting the formation of an interagency organization team that will develop minimum standards, best management practices, and other guidance materials in an effort to ensure a structured, systematic approach to LCD development.
- Advocate the development of LCDs through appropriate LCC-related organizational structures (e.g., the LCC National Council, LCC U.S. Fish and Wildlife Service Steering Committee Representatives, Regional Science Applications Assistant Regional Directors, etc.).

> *"The Refuge System has been grouping CCPs for many years—writing a single CCP that covers two or more individual refuges."*

Grouping and Coordinating CCPs and Step-Down Management Plans

The Refuge System has been grouping CCPs for many years writing a single CCP that covers two or more individual refuges. Often, the refuges grouped under one CCP are within an established administrative complex or a distinct physiographic area. The PIT recommends that this practice be enhanced under the proposed LCD paradigm:

Once an LCD is developed, the refuges within that geographic area should immediately begin developing (or revising) their CCPs. When feasible, all refuges within the geographic area covered by a single LCD should be covered under a single CCP. Doing so would be the most efficient way to step down goals and objectives from the LCD and propose refuge-specific management actions that deliver landscape-level benefits.

A number of factors may suggest that some refuges or groups of refuges within an LCD geographic area should have their own CCPs. Our ability to group refuges under a single CCP will depend on the refuges' similarities and differences in terms of habitats, species, purposes, uses, proximity, and management concerns. These and other factors will determine the degree to which refuges can be grouped under one CCP. This decision will be made on a case-by-case basis.

Even if few or none of the refuges within an LCD can be grouped under one CCP, we recommend that the development of all CCPs within an LCD should be conducted simultaneously in a coordinated manner. Refuge staff, partners, and the public would benefit from the dialogue that comes from conducting planning in a concerted manner. Shared goals, objectives, and strategies (and shared writing responsibilities for areas of overlap) could be identified. Travel costs could be reduced. Any resources saved by grouping or coordinating CCPs could be invested in future efforts to develop the step-down management plans needed to fully implement these CCPs.

Grouping step-down management plans for refuges may have similar benefits to grouping CCPs (exhibit C). Joint step-down planning for the same group of refuges covered by one CCP makes sense, because they are likely to share priorities such as species, habitats, and visitor service goals.

While individual refuges may need to add site-specific priorities, objectives, and strategies to their step-down management plans, they may be able to share much of their information with other refuges. For example, there could be multiple refuges within the same wetland complex that share similar species or conservation challenges and thus may have similar habitat management plan objectives. Planning for groups of refuges would not preclude production of separate plans to accommodate specific refuge needs.

The wetland management districts of Minnesota, for example, have already

Exhibit C: Grouping Plans under the LCD

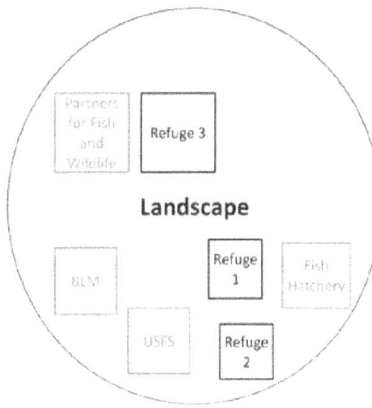

1. Multiple refuges, fish hatcheries, and partner conservation lands may be found within a landscape. Additionally, other conservation efforts (e.g. Joint Ventures) may be actively working to conserve this area. This landscape may be an entire Landscape Conservation Cooperative or a smaller area, such as an ecoregion.

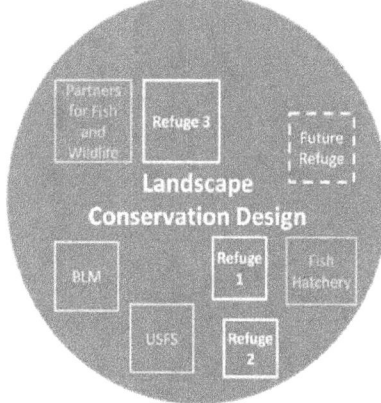

2. To be more consistent in our planning, we can set goals at this scale through a Landscape Conservation Design. This can include outlining the need for new refuges to increase connectivity or to secure specific habitat.

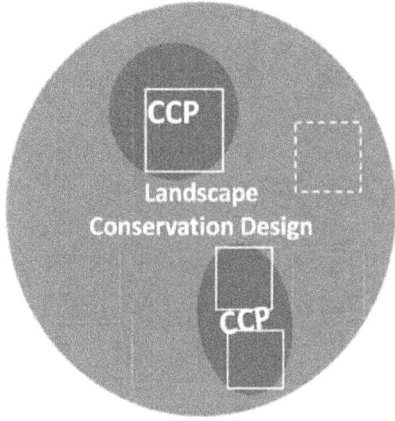

3. Comprehensive Conservation Plans (CCPs) should be written in the context of the broader Landscape Conservation Design. In theory, a CCP could encompass multiple refuges.

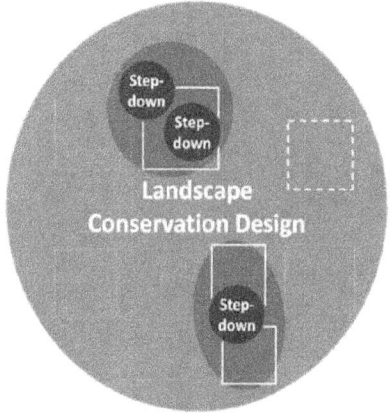

4. Just as the CCPs should tier to the larger goals in the Landscape Conservation Design, the step-down plans (including Habitat Management and Visitor Services Plans) should be directly related to their corresponding CCP. In some instances, a step-down plan may fit the needs of multiple refuges.

demonstrated that grouped planning efforts can lead to quality, individual step-down management plans. Consolidating step-down planning by coordinating efforts of multiple units would lead to more consistency among plans. The efficiency of such an approach may lead to faster development of step-down management plans without compromising their quality.

The PIT recommends that step-down management plans for all refuges within the geographic area covered by an LCD be consolidated to the maximum extent feasible.

Recommendations

- Include in a single CCP, when possible, all refuges within the geographic area covered by the LCD.
- Consolidate to the maximum extent feasible, step-down management plans for all refuges within the geographic area covered by an LCD.
- Conduct simultaneously, in a coordinated manner, development of all CCPs and (later) step-down management plans within an LCD.

> *"...it is important that each region take a leadership role in developing the LCD schedules with the LCCs within their jurisdiction."*

Establishing a Schedule for LCDs, CCPs, and LPPs

In general, our work on a CCP or LPP cannot begin until the corresponding LCD has been completed. There are three exceptions to this rule:

1. Unfinished First Round CCPs – Each region's first priority is to complete CCPs for any station where the statutory deadline for completing the initial CCP has already passed (October 9, 2012 or 15 years after the refuge was established; see Service Manual chapter 602 FW 3, "Comprehensive Conservation Planning").

2. CCPs and LPPs Already Started – Each region's second priority is to complete CCPs and LPPs that have already been started. These include plans for which (1) pre-planning is already completed or underway and (2) it is unlikely that the unit(s) will be covered under an LCD within the next three years. If an LCD is expected to begin within three years, the region should consider postponing development of the CCP or LPP until after the LCD has been completed, especially if they are in an early stage of the planning process.

3. CCPs and LPPs for Areas Outside of LCDs – In the unusual case of a Refuge System unit that is not likely to ever be covered by an LCD (for example,

an urban refuge) and is not a first or second priority for plan completion (as described above), the region should schedule the CCP or LPP for that unit in consideration of the following criteria:

*   The age or utility of the existing CCP;
*   The presence of threats to refuge resources;
*   The presence of opportunities for engagement with the public and/or partners; and
*   The existence or anticipation of a landscape-scale planning effort (other than an LCD) that could inform our CCP or LPP development.

All Other Plans

Completing the remaining CCPs and LPPs in a region should be scheduled based on that region's schedule for completing LCDs. CCPs and LPPs for all Refuge System units covered under a single LCD should be completed simultaneously, preferably within three years of the completion of that LCD.

Develop Regional and National Schedules for Completing Landscape Conservation Designs

Since regional CCP and LPP schedules will be almost entirely dependent on LCD schedules, it is important that each region take a leadership

Blazing Star; photo: USFWS

role in developing the LCD schedules with the LCCs within their jurisdiction. Regions must engage in scheduling discussions with our conservation partners at the LCC level, securing their commitments as early as possible. Since we will be working with our LCC partners to develop these schedules, we will need to reach consensus on the priority for each LCD. To the extent possible, however, we should try to prioritize LCDs that:

- contain a large number of Refuge System units;

- contain areas that may be suitable for new refuges or refuge expansions;

- contain habitat important to Service-identified surrogate species; and

- contain Refuge System units with CCPs that require revision due to their age or changed conditions.

Regional planning schedules for LCDs, CCPs, and LPPs will be compiled into a national planning schedule. This schedule will be maintained in a format that allows flexibility

for adapting to changing circumstances while providing a central source of information to share with partners and managers. This is the same approach that is currently used to maintain a CCP schedule via the national CCP database.

Recommendations

- Do not develop a CCP or LPP until the corresponding LCD has been completed, except for: (1) unfinished "first round" CCPs, (2) CCPs and LPPs that are already started, and (3) CCPs and LPPs for units in geographic areas that are unlikely to ever be covered by an LCD.

- Each region will develop CCP and LPP schedules based on the LCD schedules within their jurisdiction (see LLC and Refuge System overlay map).

- Compile regional planning schedules for LCDs, CCPs, and LPPs into a national planning schedule.

Placing Greater Priority on Step-Down Management Plans

Step-down management plans are program-specific plans that are "stepped-down" from the goals, objectives, and strategies contained in a CCP. They contain sufficient detail to guide refuge-specific programs, operations, and annual work plans. The PIT suggests that, since the development of new CCPs will be delayed pending completion of the LCDs, an opportunity exists for the Refuge System to focus on completing step-down management plans for existing CCPs.

Responses to the PIT's 2012 survey of Refuge System employees (see the Report Compendium of planning resources) revealed that most refuge personnel believe that step-down management plans are the best vehicle for implementing and monitoring CCP objectives. Greater emphasis on step-down management plans was favored by a majority (51 percent) of Refuge System employees who participated in the survey. Most respondents also expressed the concern that, at present, we do not have sufficient funds and staffing to meet planning needs. This lack of funding and planning capacity may help to explain the low completion rate of step-down management plans. For example, a recent internal review found that only about 15 percent of refuges have completed HMPs, while 4 percent have completed visitor services plans.

Step-down planning offers the opportunity to make clear connections between on-the-ground management actions and broader conservation objectives.

While each region varies in its approach to CCP and step-down planning, most agree that detailed and specific strategies are critical for implementing CCP goals and objectives. It doesn't matter whether these detailed strategies are contained in a CCP or a step-down management plan, as long as they are developed, documented, and implemented.

Several issues emerged from the PIT's evaluation of Refuge System step-down management planning, including the following:

- Refuge staffs are overwhelmed by the need to write numerous step-down management plans, with no identified priorities.

- Little training and guidance exists for writing step-down management plans.

- Each Service region has varied in its approach to the level of detail in CCPs, which affects both the level of detail needed in a step-down management plan and the level of National Environmental Policy Act (NEPA) documentation required.

- New program information is rapidly emerging (primarily from the Refuge System vision teams) that will need to be stepped-down to individual refuges.

Service Manual chapter 602 FW4, Exhibit 1, "List of Potential Step-Down Management Plans," lists approximately 40 potential step-down management plans that a refuge might need to develop. This list is not exhaustive. A refuge may need to develop another type of step-down management plan if it proposes to undertake an activity not listed in Exhibit 1. All of the step-down management plans listed in Exhibit 1 are not required on every refuge, but 10 of them are commonly stepped-down from a refuge CCP. They are:

1. Habitat Management Plan
2. Visitor Services Plan
3. Inventory and Monitoring Plan
4. Fire Management Plan
5. Cultural Resource Management Plan
6. Integrated Pest Management Plan
7. Nuisance Animal Plan
8. Furbearer or Trapping Plan
9. Wilderness Stewardship Plan
10. Land Protection Plan

Step-down management plans should have these elements:

- Begin by first developing a completion schedule.

- Track step-down management plan progress and completion on a national basis.

- Allow a flexible approach to conducting step-down planning so that each region may use different formats, documentation, and NEPA compliance, depending on the level of detail in the original CCP.

- Have an evaluation process to determine which CCPs have sufficient level of detail to satisfy step-down planning and which ones do not.

- Be based upon new guidance, training, and templates that provide efficiencies and consistency in implementing step-down planning processes across all regions. Webinars, handbooks, job aids, checklists, and training in planning from the National Conservation Training Center are examples of tools that can help guide staff for preparing of quality plans.

The schedule and steps for completing inventory and monitoring step-down management plans are described in the *"Inventory and Monitoring 7-Year Plan for the NWRS"* (April 2013). Inventory and Monitoring Plans (IMPs) are critical to the success of LCDs and are necessary to ensure that refuges have the scientific validation for making management decisions. IMPs will assist refuges in applying the adaptive management process at refuge and landscape scales. Refuges must have clear, prioritized resource management objectives before IMPs can be useful, which is why the PIT recommends

that completing HMPs be a high priority for the Refuge System.

NEPA compliance is a key consideration when planners and field staff begin the step-down planning process. Some CCPs have incorporated enough project-specific detail to allow assessment of effects under NEPA. CCPs that are more general will need to be followed by additional project/site specific step-down management plans that include NEPA analysis.

Several approaches to achieving NEPA compliance may be considered that can streamline NEPA

Prescribed fire; photo: USFWS

writing and be tailored to individual situations. For some refuge actions, a programmatic assessment that evaluates management actions (like prescribed fire or invasive species control) could cover the general effects of those actions on refuges. This type of NEPA analysis could be done with an individual refuge CCP or at a regional or national level as a precursor to step-down planning on multiple refuges. A project-specific assessment at the refuge level may still be needed, but the NEPA process and documentation (an Environmental Action Statement) would be much more condensed and simpler subsequent to a programmatic assessment. Refuges with similar needs may be able to combine their step-down management plans and associated NEPA documents. Nuisance animal control is an example where multiple refuges may have very similar actions and effects that could be completed under one step-down management plan and/or covered under one NEPA process.

Wilderness Planning

The Refuge System contains 20 percent of America's National Wilderness Preservation System (NWPS) with 20 million acres of designated wilderness on 63 refuges. The Refuge System also protects 1.9 million acres of proposed wilderness on 21 refuges. By law and policy, we are responsible for preserving the wilderness character of these designated and proposed wilderness areas. We do this, in part, by effective wilderness planning and by establishing goals and objectives in CCPs and in step-down WSPs.

Bison; photo: USFWS

Landscape-scale planning through LCDs will contain a variety of land designations including some with designated wilderness areas. Studying wilderness areas at this scale can help us understand the contributions of wilderness to wildlife conservation. Studying wilderness as part of the LCD process could also reveal issues and events that threaten wilderness character or reduce their conservation values. Wilderness areas may provide opportunities to identify surrogate species best suited for areas where management potential is modified by wilderness designation.

CCP Reporting, Tracking, and Implementation

Throughout the Refuge System, CCP implementation is tracked at the field station level with varying degrees of oversight from regional offices. Responses to the PIT's 2012 survey of Refuge System employees indicated that CCP progress is being tracked by stations in a variety of ways including informal review, annual work planning, spreadsheets, tables, and inventory and monitoring plans (see the *Report Compendium* of planning resources). Although CCPs have been completed for the majority of refuge units, no standardized tracking system to gauge CCP implementation exists. In fact, the 2012 planning survey of Refuge System employees found that one of the greatest barriers to implementing CCPs is the lack of an accurate reporting mechanism to track progress of CCP objectives (65 percent of respondents agreed). The survey also identified another major barrier to implementation station funding is not coordinated with the needs identified in CCPs (77 percent of respondents agreed).

In order to provide greater consistency in tracking CCPs across the Refuge System, the PIT recommends that the Refuge Annual Performance Plan (RAPP) be modified by adding

Photo: USFWS

a geospatial component to enable field stations to report on the extent to which their CCPs are being implemented and the contributions they are making to LCD goals. If RAPP could be fully integrated spatially the refuge would be able to track their own management efforts and monitor the actions of other partners within the LCD geographic area. Providing a geospatial component to RAPP would not only facilitate the tracking and reporting of achievements, but it would also provide valuable GIS datasets and reports that could be used by both the Refuge System and our conservation partners. Successful examples of spatially integrating management efforts includes the Habitat Information Tracking System (HabITS) database that is used by the Partners for Fish and Wildlife Program, the Refuge Habitat Management Database that has recently been used on a number of refuges in Region 1, and the Refuge System Lands Geographic Information System (RSLGIS). Ideally, a single tracking database should be used throughout the Refuge System. See the *Report Compendium* of planning resources for an example of a spreadsheet that could be used to tie CCP objectives to RAPP measures.

In addition, the PIT recommends that tracking CCP implementation should be incorporated into the Annual Performance Plans of refuge managers, project leaders, and refuge supervisors. See the *Report Compendium* of planning resources for an example of what could be incorporated into Annual Performance Plans by either creating a new critical element or incorporating the provided information into an existing element. The critical element should focus on what objectives/projects from the CCP can be achieved that year based on known staffing and funding.

Recommendations

- Develop a single database that can track every refuge's progress in implementing CCPs and contributing toward LCDs. This database should:

    - monitor the actions of other partners within the LCD geographic area;

    - have a geospatial component and should be integrated with RAPP, HabITS, RSLGIS, and/or the Refuge Habitat Management Database; and

    - incorporate CCP implementation into the Annual Performance Plans of refuge managers, project leaders, and refuge supervisors.

Improving the Scientific Quality of Refuge System Plans

Sound science should underpin every goal, objective, and strategy in every Refuge System plan. Biological, social, and economic science must be incorporated into Refuge System plans at all geographical scales. Refuge System plans should clearly communicate how the best available science was used to develop specific, measurable objectives that can be implemented to achieve our stated goals.

Several scholarly reviews have indicated that the Refuge System could incorporate more scientifically-rigorous goals, objectives, and strategies into our CCPs. The PIT's 2012 survey of Refuge System employees asked to what degree certain sections of CCPs include adequate scientific information. Refuge background descriptions, habitat management objectives, visitor services objectives, and

Water quality testing; photo: USFWS

wildlife management objectives were rated as having adequate scientific information (see the Report Compendium of planning resources). Only a little more than a third of the respondents felt landscape/multi-scale objectives adequately included scientific information.

The PIT asserts that cooperatively developing LCDs during preplanning will greatly improve the scientific quality of Refuge System plans. Planning with partners at a landscape scale and then stepping down goals and objectives to the refuge scale is a more complex process than traditional, site-specific planning. But pooling our technical resources with those of our conservation partners to develop robust LCDs will provide a firm scientific foundation for all Refuge System plans.

The PIT assembled a Science sub-team to analyze the science-related challenges of Refuge System planning and to recommend ways to meet these challenges. This sub-team's extensive findings are included in the *Report Compendium* of planning resources. The following is a brief summary of their findings.

Scientific Uncertainty and Planning

Uncertainty drives science forward, and keeps scientists looking for answers. But for natural resource managers, uncertainty can be problematic, particularly as it relates to controversial issues such as climate change. We like to have definite answers, but acquisition of perfect knowledge is generally impossible in science. So while uncertainty leads scientists to action, it can sometimes lead managers and policymakers to indecision. They may delay action in the hope of eliminating uncertainty, and/or they may use the perception of excessive uncertainty as an excuse not to make an unpopular or costly decision. Perhaps the most important notion to communicate to managers, stakeholders, and the public is that uncertainty does not equate to flawed science.

Planners and decision makers face many barriers to appropriately deal with scientific uncertainty. These barriers include: lack of funds, staff time, and/or data; lack of evidence (or awareness) that the current level of understanding is insufficient; lack of training in risk-management and/or statistics; and, occasionally, a reluctance to acknowledge the true level of uncertainty. In addition, simply defining and understanding the many types and sources of uncertainty can prove challenging.

Overcoming these barriers will require innovative responses that are tailored to the specific problem at hand. In some cases, we may require more

information from scientific research. In other cases, data may be available but synthesis and interpretation are lacking. In recognition of these challenges, the PIT Science sub-team created a number of recommendations for better addressing uncertainty, including the use of structured decision making and adaptive management. These are more fully described in the *Report Compendium* of planning resources.

Best Available Science

Over the years, there has been discussion about what is meant by "best available science" and what level of scientific rigor is appropriate for Service plans. The level of scientific rigor needed varies based on one's needs but can generally be described on a continuum from published, peer-reviewed literature to the cataloguing of local opinion or professional judgment. Here's an example of the range of information that should be sought and used:

- Scientific literature – Peer-reviewed, published works such as those in scientific journals and books.

- Gray literature – Often not peer-reviewed but may contain valuable information. Examples include technical reports, conference proceedings, government reports, and dissertations.

- Secondary data sources – Data sources that contribute to the issue or question at hand that were collected by an entity other than the one using the data, such as U.S. Bureau of Labor and Statistics, biological surveys, field notes, or other records.

- Onsite refuge data.

- Institutional knowledge/history.

- Expert opinion.

- Sound professional judgment.

- Traditional/local knowledge.

The PIT suggests that the standard for best available science will be met if our planning includes a thorough assessment of the available science, solicitation of public knowledge, careful documentation of our assumptions, and targeted monitoring to test our assumptions and enable midcourse corrections.

Recommendations

- Clearly communicate in Refuge System plans how the best available science was used to develop specific and measurable goals, objectives, and strategies.

- Base refuge-specific plans on LCDs to help ensure that every plan relies on sound biological, social, and economic science.

- Frame planning processes, documents, and staff functions around the elements of the SHC cycle of planning, design, implementation, monitoring, and research.

- Provide adequate time for planning team members to incorporate science by:

  - reducing the work responsibilities (monitoring, active management, etc.) of key refuge staff during the planning process;

  - creating a regional "floating" science position to work specifically with stations developing plans;

  - offering staff, nationwide, the opportunity to help develop plans or to temporarily assume the responsibilities of refuge staff who are occupied with planning;

  - providing funding for temporary hires during the planning process, so that they may assist with planning or take on some responsibilities of staff that are occupied with planning; and

  - training a small team of Service staff, and entrusting them with a regionwide or nationwide task or responsibility in specific situations or for topics that require specialized expertise.

- Clearly state in Refuge System plans where scientific information came from, how it was interpreted, and what assumptions were made. If available science offers more than one viewpoint or supports more than one conclusion it is important to include that information.

- Increase critical review of the science in draft plans, using both Service and outside reviewers.

- Develop and provide specific training topics for specific audiences:

  - How to read, understand, and synthesize available science to formulate science-based objectives.

  - Structured decisionmaking or similar decision tool training.

  - How to deal with scientific uncertainty.

  - Planning in the face of climate change.

  - Landscape-level planning for population and habitat objectives.

  - Monitoring and adaptive management.

  - Fundamentals of human dimensions.

- Encourage the use of standardized, Service-sanctioned metrics and indices by promoting quality existing methods or developing new methods wherever necessary (for example, methods such as the Floristic Quality Assessment or various indices of biological or ecological integrity).

- Enhance communication within the Refuge System and across all programs of the Service. Develop communication options to increase discussion and sharing of resources among planners and throughout the Service including a national planning portal with literature, resources, tools, links to secondary data, and other resources.

Standard Templates for Planning Documents

The PIT recommends that the Service develop standardized templates for CCPs, LPPs, and step-down management plans. Many people have commented that that Refuge System plans lack a consistent "look and feel." There are numerous inconsistencies among CCPs, both between and within regions (e.g., appearance, layout, topics addressed, placement of the EA, etc.).

Exhibits 4 ("*Refuge Comprehensive Conservation Plan Recommended Outline*") and 5 ("*EA or EIS Incorporating Elements of a CCP Recommended Outline*") of *Service Manual chapter 602 FW 3* contain two recommended outlines for CCPs, one for a stand-alone CCP and one for a CCP combined with an Environmental Assessment or Environmental Impact Statement. These outlines have been widely used, but they are rather sparse, given the potential complexity of our plans. Over time, each Service region has tended to develop its own templates through the sharing of documents among planners.

The PIT formed a Documents sub-team to develop a national CCP template utilizing the best practices from all regions to improve overall readability and consistency. This template is a work in progress. The PIT recommends that its authors should continue their work and that they, or other teams, should also develop templates for LPPs and step-down management plans. The PIT suggests that standardized templates would provide a consistent look and feel for Refuge System plans and facilitate plan development.

The national CCP template is intended for new CCPs and complete revisions to existing CCPs. CCPs that have already been completed will not require revision simply to match the national template. Additional guidance should be developed on how to incorporate LCD information into refuge-specific plans and how to incorporate major revisions, minor revisions, and amendments into existing CCPs.

> *"The PIT suggests that standardized templates would provide a consistent look and feel for Refuge System plans and facilitate plan development."*

Recommendations

- Continue with the development of standardized templates for CCPs.
- Develop standardized templates for LPPs and step-down management plans.
- Develop guidance on how to incorporate LCD information into refuge-specific plans and how to incorporate major revisions, minor revisions, and amendments into existing CCPs.

A Process for Reviewing and Amending CCPs

The National Wildlife Refuge System Administration Act of 1966, as amended by the National Wildlife Refuge System Improvement Act of 1997 (16 U.S.C. 668dd–668ee) states that the Secretary of the Interior shall "not less frequently than 15 years after the date of issuance of a conservation plan [CCP] . . . and every 15 years thereafter, revise the conservation plan as may be necessary." The Refuge System Administration Act further states that the Service "shall revise the plan at any time if the Secretary determines that conditions that affect the refuge or planning unit have changed significantly."

Service policy in *Service Manual chapter 602 FW 3, "Comprehensive Conservation Planning Process," states that we will* "revise the CCP every 15 years . . . or earlier if monitoring and evaluation determine that we need changes to achieve planning unit purpose(s), vision, goals, or objectives." Service Manual chapter 602 FW 3 also states that a CCP should be reviewed "at least annually to decide if it requires any revisions" and should be modified "whenever this review or other monitoring and evaluation determine that we need changes to achieve planning unit purpose(s), vision, and goals." Service Manual chapter 602 FW 3 further states that we should "document minor plan revisions that meet the criteria of a categorical exclusion in an Environmental Action Statement," and that "If the plan requires a major revision, then the CCP process starts anew at the preplanning step."

The Regional Refuge Planning Chiefs have long recognized that additional guidance for revising CCPs is needed in order to address the variety of large and small changes that a CCP may require. The planning chiefs assembled a team of Refuge System personnel in December of 2012 to provide recommendations for revisions to Service Manual chapter 602 FW 3 that would provide such guidance. This team recommended that:

- The revised policy should include definitions and procedures to address a variety of CCP revisions including "complete" revisions, "major" revisions, "minor" revisions, and "amendments." Each category of revision would require a different level of NEPA analysis. The planning chiefs' team suggested that CCPs are meant to be adaptive documents that should be able to evolve to meet changing conditions through a fairly streamlined amendment and revision process.

- Each field station could complete a questionnaire (similar to one developed by Service Region 6) to determine if their CCP needs revision. Data gleaned from the completed questionnaires would assist regional offices in prioritizing CCPs for revision, thereby facilitating the scheduling of LCDs. The questionnaire and this team's finding are included in the *Report Compendium* of planning resources.

The PIT recommends that the CCP revision guidance in Service Manual chapter 602 FW 3 be expanded, and that the revised policy should allow for the flexibility needed to address the various changes that a CCP may require in the context of landscape-level preplanning via LCDs.

A new Service Manual chapter, "Refuge Reviews" (601 FW 8) is currently under development. The current draft of this chapter describes four types of refuge reviews: comprehensive, periodic, independent, and program-specific. The comprehensive and periodic reviews will cover planning as well as staffing, employee development, budget, administration, and wildlife and habitat management. The planning component of these reviews will assess the refuge's progress and challenges in implementing the goals, objectives, and strategies contained in their refuge-specific plans and will evaluate the refuge's success in delivering landscape-level conservation through partnerships.

The periodic refuge review will be conducted for every field station (or group of stations) every five years. The periodic review will be led by a refuge chief, refuge supervisor, or assistant refuge supervisor. Depending on the size and complexity of the refuge/refuge complex, each review should take from one to four days and will generate a refuge review report in a standard format. The comprehensive refuge review will be conducted every 15 years. Preferably, the review will start immediately before the corresponding LCD so that the information generated in the review report can contribute to both the LCD and the subsequent (new or revised) CCP. Development of the comprehensive refuge review will be led by a refuge supervisor or assistant refuge supervisor with participation from the CCP planning team leader and one or more representatives from the regional office, Headquarters, other Service programs, other agencies, universities, or conservation or other organizations.

The PIT recommends that further development of Service Manual chapter 601 FW 8 should be closely coordinated with the revision of chapter 602 FW 3 and related Service Manual chapters that address planning. Specifically, the annual CCP review mentioned in chapter 602 FW 3 should be more fully described as a very limited review that consists of tracking the refuge's success in CCP implementation. This could include an update and evaluation of the CCP

tracking database and the completion of a brief CCP questionnaire, as described above. A more robust planning review could then be conducted at five-year intervals via the periodic refuge review. LCD and subsequent CCP development would be preceded by a comprehensive refuge review. The specifics of how this will be accomplished should be described in Service Manual chapter 601 FW 8.

Recommendations

- Update Service Manual chapter 602 FW 3, "Comprehensive Conservation Planning Process," and related Service Manual chapters that address planning to better address the CCP amendment and revision process.

- Coordinate the development of the new Service Manual chapter 601 FW 8, "Refuge Reviews" with the revision of Chapter 602 FW 3 and related chapters.

*Review and training;
photo: USFWS*

Policy and Training

The PIT assembled a Policy sub-team to determine if new or revised policies would be required to implement the new approach to landscape-level planning proposed in this final report. The Policy sub-team found that a number of policies would require revision. Their full report is included in the *Report Compendium* of planning resources. Their findings are summarized, below, in this sub-team report.

The PIT recommends that *Service Manual chapter 052 FW 1, "Ecosystem Approach to Fish and Wildlife Conservation"* be rewritten to serve as the new "Landscape Conservation Design" chapter. Because this chapter is applicable Service-wide policy and is not only Refuge System policy, it is essential that representatives from other Service programs be involved in its revision. This joint revision process will provide a valuable opportunity throughout the Service to consider how the LCD process can be integrated into their programs.

Service Manual chapter 601 FW 3, "Biological Integrity, Diversity, and Environmental Health," suggests the use of "historical conditions" as a frame of reference for habitat management and restoration. While this may still be a valid benchmark in many situations, it could be improved through the recognition of climate change processes and the concept of non-equilibrium ecosystems. The PIT recommends that a team of Service scientists review this policy and suggest needed changes.

The PIT further recommends that all Service Manual chapters that address planning should be revised simultaneously, by a single team. These chapters are: 602 FW 1 (*"Refuge Planning Overview"*), 602 FW 3 and Exhibits (*"Comprehensive Conservation Planning Process"*), 602 FW 4 (*"Step-Down Management Planning"*), 620 FW 1 (*"Habitat Management Plans"*), draft 602 FW 5 ("Strategic Growth"), and draft 601 FW 8 ("Refuge Reviews").

In addition to Service policy, the PIT recognizes that training may need to be developed or revised to facilitate the new approach to landscape-level planning proposed in this report. The Service should consider developing a new LCD course that would be available to both Service personnel and our conservation partners. In addition, a course or courses that focus on stepping down LCDs to refuge-specific plans are essential. As mentioned in previous sections of this report, additional training may also be needed to address step-down management plans, wilderness planning, risk management, statistics, developing science-based objectives, structured decision making, dealing with scientific uncertainty, planning in the face of climate change, monitoring and adaptive management, and human dimensions.

Staffing, Funding, and Organization

Implementing the recommendations contained in this report requires careful examination of the Refuge System's planning organization and capacity to conduct landscape-level planning. The PIT believes that many of the recommendations in this report, if implemented, will provide opportunities for streamlining our planning processes and achieving cost efficiencies. Other recommendations might increase our planning costs. This report does not directly address the Refuge System's planning organization, capacity to conduct landscape-level planning, or budget. These issues will need to be addressed if and when we move forward with each recommendation.

Responses to the PIT's 2012 survey of Refuge System employees revealed some insights that may prove useful in future evaluations of the Refuge System's capacity to conduct landscape-level planning in the manner prescribed in this report (see the Report Compendium of planning resources). Nearly two-thirds of respondents replied their station has the current staff (or access to Service staff) with the knowledge, skills, and abilities needed to plan and deliver landscape-scale conservation. Respondents identified these knowledge, skills, and abilities as: emotional intelligence, or the ability to identify, assess, manage, and control the emotions of one's self, of others, and of groups; landscape-level background and experience, including conservation biology experience, ecological knowledge, and institutional knowledge; and technical skills such as modeling, GIS, and planning. The survey results did not, however, indicate whether there are enough personnel with these skills to actually undertake the volume of work needed to accomplish landscape-level planning, Refuge System-wide.

Recommendations

- Evaluate the Refuge System's planning organization, capacity to conduct landscape-level planning, and budget— if and when we move forward with the recommendations contained in this final report. CCPs.

> *"The PIT believes that many of the recommendations in this report, if implemented, will provide opportunities for streamlining our planning processes and achieving cost efficiencies."*

> *"Refuge planning has improved how we manage our refuges and strengthened how we function as one Refuge System."*

Conclusion

The Planning Implementation Team's "Final Report: A Landscape-Scale Approach to Refuge System Planning" recommends that we focus the next generation of planning on Landscape Conservation Design, developed by the greater conservation community through partnership in Landscape Conservation Cooperatives. Our report gives an overview of the planning effort and its value and investigates how National Wildlife Refuge System planning will address large-scale conservation challenges such as climate change, while maintaining the integrity of management and conservation delivery within our boundaries.

After fifteen years of successful planning under the National Wildlife Refuge System Improvement Act of 1997, we are nearing completion of a Comprehensive Conservation Plan for every unit of the Refuge System. Refuge planning has improved how we manage our refuges and strengthened how we function as one Refuge System. While CCP planning thus far has served us well, we must take action to complete high priority step-down management plans and adapt strategies so that the Refuge System contributes to conserving functional landscapes beyond refuge boundaries. The PIT identifies and addresses the need to shift our planning to a landscape-scale approach. The recommendations in this report describe a coordinated approach to help the Refuge System more fully implement Strategic Habitat Conservation. The foundation of this approach is the LCD. Each LCD describes the partners' individual and collective goals for that landscape along with shared commitments for

implementation and monitoring. Our recommendations ensure that future planning is done with innovation, efficiency, the best available science, and with strong collaborative partnerships. They allow for flexibility in our planning and leave us poised to meet new threats and challenges that cross political and organizational boundaries.

Refuge-specific management plans include CCPs, Land Protection Plans, and a variety of step-down management plans. Under the new approach to Refuge System planning described in this report, all of these plans would address refuge-specific issues and implement the landscape-level goals and objectives identified in the corresponding LCD. Developing new CCPs and LPPs (and revising existing ones) would be postponed until the corresponding LCDs are completed. In the interim, the Refuge System would focus on completing step-down management plans to implement existing CCPs. LCDs would be developed as part of the preplanning phase of every new refuge-specific CCP and LPP. To the extent feasible, all refuges within the geographic area covered by a single LCD would be covered under a single CCP. When multiple CCPs are needed within an LCD, they would be developed simultaneously, in a coordinated manner.

Under this approach to Refuge System planning, CCPs would be broad in scope with greater detail provided in step-down management plans. Step-down management plans for all refuges within the geographic area covered by an LCD would also be developed simultaneously and consolidated. The step-down management plans that would be completed first are habitat management plans and visitor services plans. Standardized templates would be used for CCPs, LPPs, and step-down management plans. A geospatial database would be used to track every refuge's progress in implementing plans and contributing toward LCD goals. Service policy would be revised, and new training would be developed to ensure that our staff and the greater conservation community are fully prepared to implement the new approach to Refuge System planning.

Our recommendations apply only to the Refuge System, but it is our hope that other Service programs join us in basing their program-specific management plans on landscape-level goals and objectives and employ a landscape-scale conservation approach with our partners.

Report Compendium of Planning Resources

The complete *Report Compendium* of planning resources is located on SharePoint and contains the following articles and resources.

- Examples of Resources Available for Use in Landscape Conservation Design
- PIT Policy Sub-team Report
- Review of Existing Regional Templates and Other Planning Agencies
- Landscape Level Planning and the NWRS
- PIT Science Subteam Report
- Step-down Management Plans
- PIT Survey Report
- IU Paper: SMART Planning for Climate Change
- IU Paper: Private Landowner Engagement
- IU Paper: Offroad Vehicles
- IU Paper: Off-Refuge Energy Development
- IU Paper: Fragmentation Reduction
- IU Paper: Conservation Planning for the National Wildlife Refuges
- IU Paper: Climate Change in Refuges
- CCP Revision Recommendations
- LCC and Refuge System overlay map
- PIT members and contributors to PIT report

The mission of the U.S. Fish & Wildlife Service is working with others to conserve, protect, and enhance fish and wildlife and their habitats for the continuing benefit of the American people.

The mission of the National Wildlife Refuge System is to administer a national network of lands and waters for the conservation, management and, where appropriate, restoration of the fish, wildlife and plant resources and their habitats within the United States for the benefit of present and future generations of Americans.

National Wildlife Refuge System Planning:

*Conserving the Future
Recommendation #1*

Charter

Purpose

Develop guidance and processes for improving the second generation of Refuge Comprehensive Conservation Plans (CCP), and Habitat Management Plans (HMP).

The Team is responsible for researching lessons learned from the first round of CCP development, and ensuring the next round of plans consider refuges in a landscape context and describe actions to project conservation benefits beyond refuge boundaries. This Team addresses *Conserving the Future Recommendation #1.*

Sarena Selbo	Co-Chair	Headquarters Office
Will Meeks	Co-Chair	Region 6
Mike Marxen	Branch Chief, VSC	Region 1, Visitor Services
Monica Kimbrough	Nat. Res. Planner	R2 RO
Cathy Henry	Refuge Manager	Port Louisa NWR
Ken Litzenberger	Refuge Manager	SE LA Complex
Kathryn Owens	Dpty Project Leader	Back Bay NWR
Mike Dixon	Land Prot. Planner	R6 RO Planning
Winnie Chan	Refuge Planner	San Francisco Bay NWR
Ross Alliston	Refuge Planning Spec	Headquarters, Refuges
Noah Kahn	Performance Manager	Headquarters, Refuges